LONDON BUSES
around Surrey

Roy Hobbs

Ian Allan
PUBLISHING

Introduction

Details of early public transport across that part of Surrey which later came within the London Transport (LT) orbit are somewhat sketchy, though one record exists of a horse-bus service between St Johns and Woking station, which began in the latter part of the 19th century and continued for over 20 years. Another operation, referred to in an 1897 tourist guide, was of a similar service between East Horsley and Leatherhead, but no further details were provided. Around this time a Mr Wickens started the first recognised stage-carriage service in the Reigate locality, with a horse bus operating between the 'Red Cross' and Redhill station on weekdays, this eventually running half-hourly. His stables, incidentally, could still be seen in Nutley Lane, Reigate, until the early 1970s, complete with painted 'Reigate Omnibus Company' lettering. From this time on a number of operators ran a variety of services between the two towns, usually horse-drawn but including one short-lived motor-bus experiment. However, all these were but aprelude to one of the most significant events in the county's transport history.

In March 1911 Mr A. H. Hawkins, a Reigate electrical engineer, and others formed the East Surrey Traction Co Ltd (ESTC) and started a motor-bus service using two locally-bodied 30hp Leyland

Front cover: RT3725 departs South Park 'Holmesdale' and approaches Light Hill in Park Lane East with a Redhill–Reigate working on route 430 in May 1967. *Roy Hobbs*

Title page: Against the background of Reigate's Old Town Hall RML2295, a red Central Area loan, waits for the traffic lights before drawing away with a Godstone-bound working on route 410 in October 1965. At this point one-way working now applies in the opposite direction, resulting in the removal of the centre island with its distinctive lamp standard. *Roy Hobbs*

Above: Some 68 Routemaster coaches were constructed in 1962 to cater for Green Line services where passenger numbers required higher-capacity vehicles, as compared with the more usual RF single-deckers. RMC1457 passes the Friary Centre at Guildford with a 715 duty to Onslow Street bus station. *Dave Brown*

First published 2004

ISBN 0 7110 3001 4

Published by Ian Allan Publishing

an imprint of Ian Allan Publishing Ltd, Hersham, Surrey KT12 4RG.
Printed by Ian Allan Printing Ltd, Hersham, Surrey KT12 4RG.

Code: 0407/B1

single-deckers, each carrying up to 26 passengers. By the mid-1920s the company was controlling routes across a major part of Surrey, extending from Guildford and Woking in the west to the Kent towns of Sevenoaks and Tunbridge Wells in the east and from Kingston and Croydon in the north to Horsham and Uckfield, both in Sussex, in the south.

From 1921 various agreements, including those of joint working, were established with the London General Omnibus Co Ltd (LGOC), until in January 1932 the company agreed to take over those joint services operated on the LGOC's behalf by the National Omnibus and Transport Co, mainly in Middlesex and Hertfordshire. Following these changes the company adopted the title of London General Country Services (LGCS), but this was to be short lived, as, under the 1933 Act, it was compulsorily acquired by the London Passenger Transport Board (LPTB), becoming the latter's Country Department. Mr Hawkins was to remain as General Manager of this division of the new Board, eventually controlling a fleet of over 1,000 buses and coaches by the time he retired in 1946.

Strong ties were already established with chassis manufacturer the Associated Equipment Co (AEC) of Southall, via the LGOC, and together with the Board's own Chiswick facility they both continued the development of standard types to replace the older members of the fleet and a diversity of vehicles inherited from the amalgamation. These designs included the 'STL' (56-seat Regent) and the 'T' (30-seat Regal) single-decker for bus and coach use, both with Chiswick-designed bodies, which remained in continuous production until 1939. The small 20-seat single-manned 'C' type (Leyland Cub) was also introduced, to cover lightly trafficked services, mainly in the Country Area.

With the intervention of World War 2 vehicle development was put on hold, and Chiswick Works turned over to war production. However, a refined version of the 'STL' chassis, later known as the 'RT', was produced just prior to the outbreak of hostilities, and some

151 examples with an extremely modern body design had been completed by 1942 before production ceased. This design was to form the basis of the postwar double-deck fleet, and with Leyland variants eventually totalled some 6,956 examples by the time the programme was completed in 1954. Although the general introduction of the 'RM' (Routemaster), from 1959 onwards, resulted in the retirement of many of its predecessors, several lasted in service well into the late 1970s, often having completed a record 30 years of operation. A single-deck design with an underfloor engine, the 'RF' (39-seat Regal), was brought into use in 1951 and by 1953 numbered 700 examples in both bus and coach form.

The AEC Routemaster was the final design of pure London Transport (LT) parentage, and by 1968 some 2,825 had been produced for LT in both bus and coach versions, including 65 operated on behalf of British European Airways. Despite attempts to supersede it with more modern vehicles it has remained particularly suited to Central London conditions over the years. At the time of writing around 500 survive in London service, some even having returned from provincial operators after their earlier sale. However, with changed schemes of fare collection, the majority will shortly be retired, many having completed over 40 years of continuous operation.

Right: Passing the 'Angel' inn at Giggs Hill Green, Thames Ditton, RF510 is on a route 218 working to Staines in June 1978. It became one of over 100 RFs that have since passed into private hands and is now with an owner in Southport. *Geoff Rixon*

Right: This view of the rear yard at Dorking (DS) garage during June 1969 shows RT3124 along with RFs 236, 276 and 42, displaying various styles of indicator blind. All three RFs had been downgraded to bus work from Green Line duties during the mid-1960s without undergoing modernisation. Both the garage and the adjacent bus station no longer exist, the complete site being given over to residential development. *Roy Hobbs*

With the transfer of the Country Bus & Coach Department to the National Bus Company (NBC) in 1970, plus the ending of London Buses direct control by the splitting of bus operation into 11 independent units in 1988, the subsequent years have been ones of considerable change. In this album, therefore, I have sought to cover predominantly the period between 1960 and 1980, the subject being dealt with chronologically.

The county is defined as that which existed prior to 1964, before the absorption of a large area of northern Surrey by the GLC, including the Boroughs of Kingston, Sutton and Croydon. Apart from the vehicles illustrated, a number of views here provide a record of the constantly changing street scene in several locations across the county. This includes the loss of many once well-respected High Street names, along with the complete redevelopment of many town centres, as a consequence of pedestrianisation and the changes wrought by new road schemes.

My particular appreciation goes to the many photographers who have been kind enough to loan their precious transparencies for publication. These include Michael Allen, Maurice Bateman, Colin Brown, Dave Brown, Roy Denison, David Edwards, Michael Furnell, Peter Gascoine, Bruce Jenkins, Kevin McCormack, John May, Gerald Mead, Dick Riley, Geoff Rixon and James Whiting of Capital Transport.

Reference has been made to a variety of invaluable sources, in order to verify certain facts and for additional material; these include *East Surrey* (Durrant/King/Robbins, 1974); *Bus Portfolio 3: RFs* (Fennell, 1988); Capital Transport publications *London Country* (Akehurst/Stewart, 2001) and *London Buses in the 1960s* (Glazier, 1998) and various issues of *London Bus Magazine* (LOTS). Thanks are also extended to John Hambley for general advice and to David Ruddom of the London Historical Research Group of the Omnibus Society for clarifying certain points in regard to route details.

Roy Hobbs
Exeter
March 2004

During 1955 LT instituted a number of limited-stop services, mainly during rush hours, with the designation 'Express', this being displayed on the intermediate blind against a dark-blue background. These were intended to act as feeders for commuter trains to and from Central London. Route 130 was the first to introduce this type of operation in August 1955, between East Croydon and the remote satellite estate at New Addington. Other services appeared later that year with routes 93 (Epsom–Morden) and 403 (Chelsham–West Croydon); these were followed in May 1956 by route 406A (Kingston–Tattenham Corner, extended to Tadworth that December). RT4262, with a Saunders body, awaits its next turn of duty at East Croydon during October 1955. *Bruce Jenkins*

Below: Amongst a number of routes operating lowbridge-type vehicles was the 127 (South Wimbledon–Morden Station). RLH67 of Merton (AL) garage is seen having passed under the offending structure at Worcester Park station during August 1958. The only Central Area route south of the Thames that required the use of this particular type, the 127 was withdrawn in 1958 following a long busmen's strike and not reinstated. The RLH class was introduced on this service in 1952, replacing the similarly low-height utility D (Daimler CWA6) type. The operating career of RLH67 ended with its disposal to a Yorkshire breaker in September 1972. *Bruce Jenkins*

Right: The 215 was the last of several routes operating from Kingston (K) garage that employed postwar TD (Leyland Tiger PS1) single-deckers. Originally numbering 131, they were a stop-gap design introduced by LT in 1946 to replace various single-deck types of prewar design that had been retained due to the outbreak of hostilities. By 1959/60 the great majority of the TDs had been withdrawn, being superseded by the later RF class. However, this was not possible on route variation 215A, due to restrictions on vehicle length. Approval was subsequently granted in early 1962 for use of the longer RF, and the TDs were finally replaced on 28 February 1962. TD129 is pictured at the Cobham terminus on 22 July 1961. *Gerald Mead*

Left: On its way to Kingston, RT849 is seen in Walton Road, East Molesey, with a route 131 duty in April 1962, shortly before partial conversion to RM operation. In recent times the route has undergone a variety of changes, in the form of both extensions and cutbacks at each end, but currently runs between Kingston and Wimbledon only, no longer serving East or West Molesey; it is now the responsibility of London United's Fulwell garage. In 1962 the intermediate blind was still displaying upper-case lettering, then in the process of being superseded. The lady's bicycle, complete with chaincase, is worthy of note and would be quite a rare vintage specimen today! *Geoff Rixon*

Above: During the final week of trolleybus operation, in May 1962, 'L3' No 1528 makes its way from Surrey into Middlesex as it crosses the River Thames at Kingston on its evening return to Fulwell depot on route 604. The 'L3' class was introduced to the Kingston-area routes — the last to be converted — from January 1961 as a consequence of the sale of Fulwell's postwar 'Q1' class to municipalities in northern Spain, which required early delivery of these modern vehicles to upgrade their own systems. The Kingston routes had been the first to introduce this form of traction to London, from May 1931, when the original vehicles, known as 'Diddlers', were brought into service by London United Tramways, replacing earlier tram routes. *Roy Hobbs*

Below: As recorded earlier, replacement of the trolleybus routes in the Kingston area — the last to disappear under the LT scheme which had commenced in March 1959 — eventually took place on 8 May 1962. In this view one of the Routemasters that took over is shown under the abandoned overhead system opposite Surbiton station. Brand-new RM1114, on its first day in service, 9 May 1962, is seen on route 281 (replacing trolleybus route 601), turning from Claremont Road into St Mark's Hill on its journey to Tolworth. Note the route number displayed on the rear staircase panel, a design feature later discontinued. RM1114 would eventually be sold to Yorkshire breakers in June 1990. *Geoff Rixon*

Right: Close to the end of its career with LT, RT137, one of the original batch of RTs built in 1940, is seen at the temporary terminus of route 406 at Tattenham Corner on Derby Day in June 1962. It is probably serving as a control point for inspectors supervising the turnaround and loading of buses on this route and may also have played host to engineering staff, required to deal with any related problems. RT137 was one of seven painted green for passenger service on route 327 in Hertford, their low overall weight allowing their use over a weak bridge at Broxbourne. On replacement by postwar RTs in September 1957 they were allocated to staff duties or the training fleet. RT137 operated from Reigate (RG) garage on the former until transfer to driver-training there in September 1959. Final withdrawal came in February 1963, by which time it was among the last of the first series still in use. *Peter Gascoine*

Left: The 'Holmesdale' public house in South Park lay south of Reigate and during the 1920s and 1930s was the terminus at times for East Surrey routes S21 and S29, originating variously from South Merstham or Reigate. On what was a rather unusual working, red lowbridge RLH52 arrives from Reigate with a route 430 duty in June 1962. The distinctive blind layout is worthy of note. The RLH was probably acting as a replacement for the usual RT on Derby Day, when all available vehicles of the latter type would be required for the 406F special service between Epsom station and Epsom Downs. RLH52 would normally have been employed on peak-hour duties between Redhill and South Merstham on route 447, on which two low railway bridges necessitated its use. Regrettably, the 'Holmesdale' would be demolished in the 1990s to make way for 'executive' housing. *Roy Hobbs*

Above: Onslow Street bus station in Guildford on 31 January 1964, with Guy Special GS21 departing with a Peaslake journey on route 448. The 84 buses of the one-man-operated GS class were first brought into service during 1953, mainly to replace the prewar C class (Leyland Cub) on lightly-trafficked rural routes in London Transport's Country Area. This route is of interest inasmuch as it was the result of a rare working agreement between LPTB and Tillingbourne Valley Services Ltd, following creation of the former in 1933. However, both the route and some of the vehicles eventually passed to Tillingbourne in August 1964, when London Transport gave up its share of the operation. *Bruce Jenkins*

One unfortunate consequence of the rapid replacement of ageing stock by LT following the end of World War 2 was its virtual completion by the early 1950s, with the result that several significant types (in the history of London's bus development) were lost before the private preservation movement had got into its stride. Fortunately, a number have now been reclaimed from subsequent uses as staff transports, caravans, etc, which has filled certain gaps, though some still exist. One saved privately is pictured here at Petridgewood Common, South Earlswood, during May 1965 on the HCVC run to Brighton. This is 'Tunnel' STL1871, one of 40 with a specially contoured roof profile allowing them to work through the Rotherhithe and Blackwall tunnels on routes 82 and 108. There would, however, be a sad end to the story; although partially restored to prewar livery, this (by then) unique vehicle would be sold for scrap in November 1967, due to the owners' difficulty with storage and ongoing restoration costs. *Roy Hobbs*

A resplendent RT549 departs West Croydon bus station on a route 133 duty to Hendon Central during October 1965. Note once again the use of upper-case lettering on the intermediate blind, this having generally been replaced by lower-case from 1961 onwards. RT549 was originally fitted with a body with a roof-mounted route-number box, but this has been replaced during the course of routine overhaul. Body interchanges were a normal feature of London Transport's overhaul procedures at Aldenham Works, where body and chassis were separated and dealt with individually on a production-line basis, enabling those most recently completed to be united, thereby speeding up the process.
Maurice Bateman

Before the town's one-way scheme was introduced in 1968, brand-new RML2305 on route 410 passes XF7 on the 424 stand at Reigate 'Red Cross' during October 1965. The RML was one of the 17 red vehicles loaned over the October/November period following the scheduled changeover to the type at Godstone (GD) garage on the 409/410/411 group of routes, insufficient green vehicles having come off the production line by the transfer date. The XF was one of eight being trialled at East Grinstead (EG) garage, mainly on route 424, although there were occasional appearances on other routes. The 'Albion' public house on the left-hand side of this view was later demolished to permit alterations to the road layout, and, along with adjoining land, the vacant site was then used to meet the demand for increased car-parking facilities in the town. *Roy Hobbs*

During the immediate postwar era and well into the 1950s, before car ownership became widespread, it was common practice, especially at weekends, for Central Area garages to loan vehicles to the Country Area. At such times considerable extra demand was placed on certain routes by people wishing to leave Central London and its suburbs to enjoy some recreation in country surroundings. This was in addition to the Central Area routes extended into country locations during the summer timetable for similar reasons. Route 93 was one such, being extended from Epsom to Dorking and only ceasing in the summer of 1960. One of the last loans to the southern half of the Country Area, albeit due more to vehicle shortage, was of two red RTs from Croydon (TC) garage, which Reigate (RG) operated — mainly on local route 430 — for around three months between February and April 1966. RT1719 is seen approaching the 'Holmesdale' stop at South Park with a Redhill journey. *Roy Hobbs*

17

RLH45 waits at Sheerwater Estate, near Woking, with a school working on route 420 (Woking–West Byfleet Station) in April 1966; whilst required predominantly for routes 436, 436A, 461 and 463, the type was (through interworking) employed occasionally on routes normally scheduled for RT operation. The Guildford- and Addlestone-based examples would be the last of their type in service with LT's successor, London Country, finally being replaced in August 1970 — seven months after that company's formation — by one-man-operated single-deck SM (AEC Swift) vehicles.
Maurice Bateman

During the late 1960s LT carried out in-service trials with 'off-the-peg' rear-engined vehicles of the XF (Daimler Fleetline) and XA (Leyland Atlantean) classes, to establish which was the more suitable for one-person operation (OPO). The eight XFs were painted green and allocated to East Grinstead (EG) garage, where they were used predominantly on route 424 (East Grinstead–Reigate), but in 1966 they spent three months working in the Central Area on route 271 (Highgate–Moorgate), a similar number of red XAs being loaned to East Grinstead for similar evaluation on the 424. In the event, the Fleetline was chosen for LT fleet replacement. XA44 approaches the Bell Street, Reigate, stop with an East Grinstead working during May 1966. Incidentally, the property behind the bus has been used both as a dental practice and, latterly, as solicitors' premises, both of which your author has had cause to use!
Roy Hobbs

Left: One of the lesser-known routes on which the RLH type was to be found was the 447, running between Redhill and South Merstham and normally operated by RF single-deckers. However, these were found to be inadequate for peak-hour traffic, and a few journeys were worked by an RLH. As is apparent from this view, its use was dictated by the usual problem of low bridges, that illustrated being one of a pair located in Battlebridge Lane, Merstham. RLH27, seen in April 1966, was allocated to Reigate garage from November 1963 and, apart from a two-month absence at Godstone, continued on the service until the low-height requirement ceased, in December 1967. Subsequently exported to the USA, it was last reported as an antique-furniture store in South Carolina in 1978. *Maurice Bateman*

Left: On an obviously very warm summer's day, if the various windows are any guide, RT4501 waits on the 'Red Cross' stand in Reigate during June 1966 with a route 430 duty to Redhill. It is one of the second batch of Green Line RTs introduced in 1954, specifically for the 723 group of routes operated by Grays (GY) garage between Tilbury and Aldgate. Following their replacement by RCL-type Routemasters, in June 1965, they were distributed around the remaining Country Area garages, where they could be used on normal bus work or on Green Line relief duties, as necessary. All of those constructed for coach use were standard vehicles, other than being fitted from new with saloon heaters, which items had yet to be adopted on the remainder of the fleet. *Roy Hobbs*

The well-known riverside terminus alongside the former GWR Staines West railway station in July 1966, with green lowbridge RLH21 on route 461 accompanied by RT2833 on route 90 and an unidentified RF on either the 216 or the 218. The station site is no longer used, most services now terminating at a central bus station. The routes themselves have also changed, the 90 having been withdrawn and the 461 commencing at Woking (rather than Staines) and now running through to Kingston; this, along with routes 216 and 218, is now operated by Tellings-Golden Miller from its Fulwell depot. RLH21 was exported to Virginia, USA, in 1975, later moving to California, but has not been traced further since October 1981. *James Whiting*

A deserted Onslow Street bus station in Guildford, with its basic passenger shelters, on New Year's Day 1967, with a lonely RLH26 awaiting custom on route 436. RLH26 was from the second batch, delivered in 1952, of which 32 were allocated initially for Country Area routes and 24 for those in the Central Area. The 436 had its origins in a route run by independent operator J. R. Fox in 1929; this company was acquired by East Surrey in 1931, when the route became the 36, at that time running between Guildford and Woking. Sometime after June 1933 it was extended first to Windsor and then, in July 1935, to Uxbridge, by which time it had been renumbered 436. However, by June 1938 the route had been cut back to Staines, which remained the terminus until June 1981. RLH26 was exported to Hawaii in 1972 and is believed to have been scrapped in 1984. *Roy Denison*

RT3843 draws away from its penultimate stop at Lower Kingswood 'Fox' and heads towards the right-hand turn into Buckland Road, leading to route 80's terminus at the 'Mint Arms'. The landscape has altered considerably since this view was recorded in March 1967: the A217 road at this point has been widened to a dual carriageway (and now provides a link to the M25 and Gatwick Airport), resulting in the elimination of both the blue Police and red telephone boxes, along with the adjacent warning-siren post. A scheme for the route's takeover by LGCS and to extend it two miles south to Reigate, in June 1932, was thwarted by union opposition at the LGOC's Sutton (A) garage; some 50 years later, in April 1982, its successor route 280 was replaced by London Country's 422 from Redhill, which continues to operate as route 420 with the blue-and-yellow vehicles of Metrobus. *Roy Hobbs*

Above: Shortly after setting out from Tadworth station on its journey towards Esher through Surrey's rural byways, RF695 crosses local heathland as it approaches Walton-on-the-Hill in March 1967. Like a number of the county's rural routes, this particular through service did not survive in its original form, being first diverted from Tadworth to terminate at Boxhill (M-F), in June 1974, and later withdrawn between Leatherhead and Esher, in November 1975. The current service is the 516 (Epsom–Dorking), which runs via Leatherhead and Betchworth station. One of the final batch of the 700 RFs built, having been completed in November 1953, RF695 was fitted with platform doors. These were a luxury initially denied its Central Area counterparts, on account of Metropolitan Police regulations (later rescinded), but an absolute necessity in a country winter! *Roy Hobbs*

Right: A view at Leatherhead (LH) garage recorded one Sunday during March 1967, when the majority of its RT fleet was parked up, awaiting return to work the following day. Red RT4296 is on route 65A to Ealing (Argyle Road), the letter suffix indicating a Saturday and Sunday extension to Leatherhead from the usual weekday terminus at Chessington Zoo. RT981, on the extreme left of the RT group, would be one of the last to survive with LCBS, not being withdrawn until February 1978. The garage was demolished in 1999 and has since been replaced by office accommodation. *Roy Hobbs*

Derby Day in June 1967, with RTs 979 and 3145 on the special 406F (Epsom Station–Epsom Downs) service. Until 1963 a similar service (406E) had operated from Epsom Town, but this ceased, due presumably to traffic congestion in the town centre. RT979 is of interest inasmuch as it still wears Green Line livery, complete with bullseye motif. Green Line RTs had first been introduced in 1950, replacing earlier Ds and STLs operating on routes 721, 722 and 726 run by Romford (RE) depot to Aldgate bus station in the City. RT979 was from a later batch of 28 introduced for Green Line relief duties from various garages. The 406F continues to run on Derby Day, currently being in the hands of London General, and is still well patronised, thanks largely to the obvious parking restrictions now in force on this important day in the racing calendar. *Roy Hobbs*

A further service run by LT to Epsom on race days is an unnumbered 'Express' from Morden Underground station. Displaying a rather crumpled blind sticker, RT1978 of Merton (AL) garage waits to cross the main A240 road into Great Tattenhams on Derby Day 1967. In the period immediately following World War 2 a large collection of vehicles from the reserve fleet, most awaiting withdrawal, ended their days on this service.

Around 140 — predominantly ST, LT and STL types — were observed on Derby Day 1949, running from a variety of garages right across the whole of LT's Central Area, sometimes with clouds of steam emanating from their overheated engines, after tackling the final steep gradient of Longdown Lane with a full load, before reaching the original Buckle's Gap terminus. *Roy Hobbs*

Left: In the original Crawley bus station in June 1967 we find RT3459 on local Ifield service 426A together with Southdown 1206, a Plaxton-bodied Leyland Leopard, on an unidentified duty. A 'Queen Mary' Leyland PD3/4 can be glimpsed to the rear, probably on Southdown route 23. Crawley's bus services would be restructured on 24 April 1971, when the majority of Southdown's local routes passed to London Country and were integrated into the latter's network. Although some new routes, serving ongoing housing developments, were introduced later, this would remain largely unchanged until a revised scheme, C-Line, was brought into effect in July 1978. The bus station seen here has now been submerged by a large shopping mall. *Roy Hobbs*

Above: Several services into Surrey were operated from the small Crawley (CY) garage in West Sussex, just over the original county boundary near Lowfield Heath. In this view, recorded one Sunday in June 1967, a line-up of RTs plus a Green Line RF await the call of duty on the following day. The route numbers displayed are of interest insofar as most no longer exist or have been redesignated. Route 853, together with its variants, was the last of a small group in the '85x' series that were allocated to the Southern Division of the Country Area, finally being withdrawn in December 1967 and replaced by others in the '4xx' series. Green Line route 710 was similarly withdrawn in November 1968 but not replaced, whilst route 405 is now within the London 'red bus' network, currently running between Croydon and Redhill and operated by Metrobus, as are most other routes based at Crawley. The garage was replaced in 1981 by a larger depot close to Gatwick Airport. *Roy Hobbs*

Left: In the kind of snowy conditions seldom found in southern England in these days of climate change, RT3202 makes its way up Light Hill in Park Lane East, shortly after leaving South Park 'Holmesdale', on its way to Reigate in the winter of 1968. Route 430 linked several local communities to the south of Reigate and Redhill, as well as serving the main hospital, and was extended to Merstham over the 447 route on Sundays, when RFs were used. Metrobus currently operates this as daily route 435 (Reigate–Merstham), the original number now applying to a shortened variation. RT3202 would be one of 34 Country Area RTs returned to the Central Area in the summer of 1972 and one of the last RTs to work from Bromley (TB) garage before Routemasters took over in August 1978. *Roy Hobbs*

Below: RF573 heads down Bridge Street, Leatherhead, towards the LT garage, with a route 462 journey for Addlestone during September 1968. Of note are the elderly street lamps, probably converted from gas lighting. This service originated in 1926 as LGOC route 162B, then running through to Staines and Slough. On passing to the LPTB in 1933 it was renumbered 462 and was subsequently operated by five C type from Windsor (WR) garage. In the immediate postwar period former Green Line 9T9 AEC Regal coaches, built in 1936, were employed due to replacement by the more advanced 10T10 design. Around 1966/7 the basic route was cut back to Addlestone, with the odd journey running to Chertsey. RF573 is amongst the large number of its type now preserved and was last recorded with a Wimbledon owner. *Michael Allen*

Above: Addlestone town centre, with RLH34, based at Guildford (GF) garage, having just made it through the lights at the junction of High Street and Station Road on route 436 sometime during September 1968. RLH34 was one of the second batch of this class of 76 vehicles first introduced in 1950 to replace a variety of elderly lowbridge types — some dating as far back as 1930 — still operating over various parts of the London Transport system. Addlestone (WY) and Guildford garages were responsible for a group of routes using Staines as one terminus, which entailed negotiating a low railway bridge just outside the town. As recorded earlier, the problem was overcome in 1970 when OPO single-deck vehicles were substituted, by which time the routes in question had become the last Country routes to be RLH-operated, albeit by then under the auspices of LCBS. *Michael Allen*

Right: As pedestrians make use of the zebra crossing, RT1360 approaches the well-known Purley crossroads in September 1968 with a route 197 journey to Caterham Valley. This Saunders-bodied vehicle is fitted with a roof-mounted route-number box, sometimes referred to as a 'lighthouse' by staff and employed on the first 750 RTs delivered postwar, as well as on later buses bodied by Saunders and Cravens; subsequent deliveries from Park Royal and Weymann had the route number repositioned alongside the intermediate display. Being of older construction and non-standard, the roofbox RTs were the first to be sold on, the last leaving the fleet in the early 1970s. Many found further service, often with provincial operators. Route 197 would eventually be succeeded by the 407, this now being in the hands of Arriva London and operating between Caterham Valley and Sutton via Croydon. *Michael Allen*

During September 1968, following a disastrous flood at Leatherhead garage, the majority of the allocation became inoperative, with the consequence that a number of red Central Area vehicles had to be drafted in temporarily. In this view RT2143 from Catford (TL) garage waits at the Ashley Road traffic lights in Epsom prior to turning into the High Street with a 406 duty from Redhill to Kingston. As with many other large towns throughout the county, a central one-way system now operates, and it is no longer possible to proceed northbound at this point. A number of alterations have been made to cope with the south- and westbound traffic, and Reid's store has since been demolished. *Michael Allen*

A further red RT brought in during the Leatherhead flood crisis was RT3086 of Peckham (PM) garage, shown awaiting the return of its driver at the Bookham Station terminus of route 418 before collecting waiting passengers and heading for Kingston. This is believed to have been the last instance of red Central Area vehicles being loaned to the Country Area, which practice had been commonplace at weekends in the immediate postwar years, until the advancement of private motoring through the late 1950s and subsequently made this no longer necessary. *Michael Allen*

RML2663 negotiates a hilly stretch of Godstone Road near Purley in January 1969 with a route 197 working to Caterham town, described here as Caterham Valley to distinguish it from nearby Caterham-on-the-Hill, then served by Country Area routes 409, 411 and 440. During the week the 197 was normally the preserve of the RT type, but on Sundays, as here, it was worked by RMLs from Croydon (TC) garage. From January 1974 one-person operation (OPO) was introduced with the use of the DMS type throughout the week. *Michael Allen*

Route 408 was originally East Surrey route S6B, having been introduced in November 1921 between Epsom and Guildford, with later extensions to Sutton and West Croydon. In recent years various route rationalisations have seen it cut back, firstly from Guildford to Leatherhead and latterly from West Croydon to Sutton and then Epsom. Currently operation is in the hands of Epsom Buses, trading as Quality Line, with the service now extended to Cobham via Oxshott. On the original route, RT3145 is seen east of Leatherhead on its way to Guildford in January 1969.
James Whiting

Above: A snowy Station Road East, in the small town of Oxted, is the location for RML2348 on a route 410 working to Bromley North station on 8 February 1969. From April 1934 this route had a dedicated fleet of 12 lowbridge vehicles, known as 'Godstone STLs', being AEC Regents with purpose-built bodies by Weymann. These were replaced from 1950 onwards by the RLH type, illustrated earlier. A low railway bridge at Oxted dictated their use, but in June 1966 the problem was resolved by lowering the road under it, permitting the use of normal-height vehicles through the town centre. A couple of formerly well-known High Street names — Achille Serre and Fine Fare — are evident in this scene.
Michael Allen

Right: Old Coulsdon is around 1½ miles from Coulsdon and in April 1969 was the terminus of route 190 from Thornton Heath. RT3949 is seen working through the town centre, where the distant overbridge, adjacent to Smitham station, still carried an original 'Southern Electric' sign giving the directions to this and nearby Coulsdon North Station. The destination blind showing intermediate points is again of interest due to the upper-case lettering employed, such blinds having generally been replaced with lower-case versions from 1961 onwards.
Michael Allen

Below: A short working on route 414 from West Croydon to Capel, recorded outside the 'Red Lion' in Coulsdon during April 1969. This route, over its full length to Horsham, was the longest in the Country Area. A variety of 'red' and 'green' routes passed through Coulsdon at this time, including the 166 to the Chipstead Valley and the Green Line 710 on its way from Amersham to Crawley. The conductor appears to have his hand on the bell cord as the driver of RT671 waits to pull away. The National Provincial Bank is another example of those High Street names that have disappeared, having been absorbed into the NatWest empire. *Michael Allen*

Right: Another long route in the Country Area's Southern Division was the 470, originating in Chelsham, close to the Kent border. It had its origins in LGOC route 70D (Morden–Dorking) and, following the formation of the LPTB in 1933, was unusual in being jointly worked by both Central and Country areas as route 70. In 1939 this pattern was altered, the basic Central Area portion becoming route 93 (Morden–Epsom), whilst the Country section became route 470 and was diverted at Ewell to serve West Croydon, this later being extended to Warlingham and Chelsham. RT4048 leaves the 'White Horse' stop in Dorking and heads for the bus station in April 1969. The original facade of the Woolworth's store will be noted. *Dave Brown*

Left: As the caravans and mobile homes congregate in the dip alongside Epsom Racecourse's finishing straight prior to Derby Day in June 1969, RT3862 stands at the terminus of route 164A at Tattenham Corner. As a result of the huge crowds massing by the racetrack at this location, the terminus was moved around 200 yards further east into Great Tattenhams on Derby and Oaks days. This point is no longer a terminus, as from March 1979 the 164A was replaced by a diversion of route 280A, itself succeeded in April 1982 by London Country route 420, covering the greater part of its route to Sutton. Following further route adjustments the 420 is now operated by Metrobus, as mentioned earlier. *Roy Hobbs*

Above: A further view at Dorking, taken across the garage forecourt during June 1969, this being the terminus for various routes, including the two RF-operated Green Line services, 712 and 714, running to Dunstable and Luton respectively. There was once a service 713, which also ran to Luton but via Victoria rather than Baker Street. However, in May 1975 both routes ceased to run south of London, being replaced by route 703 to Dorking, itself succumbing to withdrawal in October 1976. Until the introduction of RFs in 1952 the original services had been worked by the distinctive underfloor-engined TF (Leyland Tiger FEC) coaches, these being the only examples running south of the Thames; TF77, the sole survivor, is now in the care of London's Transport Museum. *Roy Hobbs*

Above: Following the withdrawal from passenger service, in 1968 and 1966 respectively, of the two Leyland variations of the RT class — the RTL and the 8ft-wide RTW — several RTWs were employed on driver-training duties, some being allocated to Country Area garages. RTW154 waits to join the busy A217 from Lesbourne Road, Reigate, whilst on one such duty from Leatherhead garage in August 1969. The buildings in the background were formerly the offices of the East Surrey Traction Co (previously two private houses), the original garage premises being evident to their rear; both have long since given way to a modern office development. Many examples of both RTL and RTW types were exported to Sri Lanka, where they enjoyed a few more years of service in the capital, Colombo. *Mike Harries*

Right: Before undertaking the long cross-country run to East Grinstead, RF690 waits at route 434's West Sussex terminus at Horsham (Carfax) on 25 July 1970. Its journey, via Crawley, will take it through various Sussex communities, with a brief incursion into the Surrey countryside at Felbridge near East Grinstead. Although by now belonging to London Country, RF690 still retains LT's standard Country Area livery for the type, complete with the well-known bullseye symbol, the only significant difference being its new owner's fleetname. *Michael Allen*

Below: At the opposite end of route 434, recorded on the same date as the picture on the previous page, is this view of the LCBS garage at East Grinstead (EG), latterly the most southeasterly destination for Country Area bus operations and adjoining mainly Maidstone & District territory. Of interest is the cautionary notice on the garage doors, probably dating from the early 1930s, when open-top vehicles were used on regular services alongside their covered-top cousins. RF209, with blinds set for route 435, is one of 175 Green Line vehicles upgraded in 1966/7 (being treated to substantial internal refurbishment, twin headlamps and a revised paint scheme) to present a more modern image, whilst RF388 is one of several red examples loaned to the Country Area and LCBS during the 1960s and 1970s to cover vehicle shortages. The garage would eventually be closed in December 1981. *Michael Allen*

Right: An early Routemaster, RM391, makes its way along Chipstead Valley Road, near Coulsdon, on 31 August 1970 with a route 59 working to the terminus at the 'Midday Sun' public house in Chipstead village. This route has a considerable history, having a long association with the Croydon area and was first run, mainly as a Summer Sunday service, by the LGOC from Camden Town to South Croydon in 1912. Its southern terminus varied over the years as it became a weekday service and included Reigate, Caterham and Godstone, as well as Chipstead, some services bearing letter suffixes to distinguish them from the parent route. From 1916 these were in the control of Thomas Tilling. The 59 commenced as a daily service to Reigate in 1923 and in this form lasted until 1930, whereafter it became a Summer Sunday and Bank Holiday operation only; this finally ceased on Sunday 2 October 1933, thereby becoming the last 'red bus' route to work into the town from Central London. *Michael Allen*

Purley Cross, the well-known junction of the A23 and A22, together with other connecting roads, is illustrated here on 31 August 1970, with passengers boarding RF510 on a route 234B working to Selsdon from South Croydon garage; this was a Sunday-only variation of route 234, which ran on weekdays from Selsdon to Hackbridge. Although the junction has been extensively redesigned in recent years, it still presents a considerable problem for rush-hour traffic, local news bulletins regularly featuring reports of hold-ups on weekdays. RF510 would be one of the final members of its class to be withdrawn, at Kingston (K) garage in March 1979. *Michael Allen*

As the driver resets the blind, RT3251 waits to commence the return journey from the rural terminus of the 'Harrow' at Farleigh, near Chelsham, with a route 470 working to Dorking on 31 August 1970. At the time this was one of two separate termini for routes 408 and 470 plus short workings of the 403 (as 403B), the other being Warlingham Park Hospital (here 403A). From 3 July 1971 these two points were linked by Harrow Road, the hospital then becoming the final destination; at the same time the 403 suffix letters were discontinued, the route no longer running beyond Chelsham through to Tonbridge. The 408 and 470 were later cut back to West Croydon, and in August 1980 the latter was effectively withdrawn, apart from two schoolday journeys, the greater part of its route being covered thereafter by the 408, which still operates today in revised form. Farleigh and the Great Park (formerly the hospital) are now served by Metrobus routes 409 and 411. *Michael Allen*

49

With the reintroduction of trams to Croydon in May 2000, this scene outside East Croydon station has been radically altered, its frontage and approach road having been remodelled, and a section of carriageway extending along George Street given over to tramway operation. In this view, recorded one Sunday in November 1970, RT3977 on route 12 and RT4651 heading for Forest Hill on the Sundays-only 194C proceed through an abnormally quiet Croydon, which would seldom be the case today with widespread Sunday opening. Neither route currently exists in this form, the surviving 194 having been cut back from Forest Hill to Sydenham, whilst the 12 no longer runs through to Shepherd's Bush, only a section being covered by route 312 from South Croydon to Peckham. *Michael Allen*

Kingston Bridge, with the famous Surrey department store of Bentalls visible in the distance; evidence of the latter's considerable size is provided by the roof-mounted signs visible either side of approaching RT4054, heading for West Molesey on route 131 on 20 March 1971. Also of interest is the little three-wheel milk float of LCS Dairies making its leisurely way across the bridge and, no doubt, impeding other traffic in the process! Considerable alterations have since been made to the town's road layout, to improve traffic flow through its sometimes constricted streets, and a number of buildings in the area behind the tree in the middle distance have been demolished to allow a better road alignment on the approach to the Wood Street one-way system. *Michael Allen*

The rather stormy sky and damp road surface suggest the passing of a recent shower, but the latter is probably the work of the local water company undertaking maintenance! Here red RF374, on loan to LCBS, negotiates a right-hand turn at Flanchford, near Leigh, with a short working of service 425 from Redhill to Dorking late one afternoon in February 1971. Of the former Central Area RFs loaned to LCBS at this period, RF374 was the sole example allocated to Dorking garage. This section of route is not served today other than by the two daily Post Bus services. *Roy Hobbs*

Right: Designed in conjunction with LT engineers, the CR (Leyland REC) was a development of the 20-seat Leyland Cub and a revolutionary design embodying an in-line rear-mounted engine. The prototype appeared in 1937, but the majority of this 49-strong class were constructed in 1939, when, as a result of the outbreak of hostilities, they were soon put into storage, having seen little service. From 1946 they were used on Central Area peak-hour relief duty, assisting the severely run-down wartime fleet. However, a small number were used to establish new Country Area routes, and two were allocated to East Grinstead garage for use on route 494 to Oxted, being among the last to operate in regular service, in 1953. Unlike the majority, these were green and included CR14, here preserved in red livery and seen crossing Petridgewood Common, South Earlswood, on the A23 while participating in the HCVC run to Brighton in May 1971. *Roy Hobbs*

Right: Although Hampton Court and its well-known palace were considered part of Middlesex prior to absorption by the GLC, an anomaly existed whereby Hampton Court railway terminus, on the other side of the River Thames, was in Surrey. RF343 waits on the station forecourt in September 1971 with a route 206 working to the former rural outpost of Claygate; currently this dormitory village is served by route K3, operated with low-floor Dennis Darts by London United and running between Esher and Roehampton Vale. RF343 was converted to enable one-person operation in January 1965 but lacks the usual Pay As You Enter advice normally located below the windscreen on the nearside. *Colin Brown*

Before the pedestrianisation of Redhill town centre RT3053 makes its way along Station Road past Redhill station with a special working on route 410 to Biggin Hill for the annual Air Display on 18 September 1971. From the destination details it would appear to be taking up the northerly section of route on arrival, as this is normally split into two sections on these occasions due to traffic congestion. All buildings visible here have now disappeared to make way for an extensive complex including shops, a bus station, library, theatre and multi-storey car park, resulting in various road closures and diversions. *Michael Allen*

A further view of Redhill town centre, recorded on the same date as the previous picture, before the complete elimination of through road traffic. Most of the shops seen here remain, although the main building, of which Boots forms a part, and the adjacent car park to the rear have been redeveloped into a large shopping mall, the 'Belfry Centre', in similar fashion to so many other locations in suburban Surrey. RML2354 is shown on a route 410 short working from Biggin Hill, covering the route's southern section on Air Display day, the blind having now been reset for the return journey. *Michael Allen*

Left: Having surmounted the steep High Street climb in Sutton, RT2199 of Sutton (A) garage commences its turn into Cheam Road at the traffic lights by the 'Cock Inn', on its way to Kingston on route 213A early in 1972. This route variation allowed for Sunday journeys to Belmont, via Carshalton, rather than the more usual terminus at Sutton garage. The 213 was originally a single-deck route, TD-class Leyland PS1s often being used during the immediate postwar period to replace the elderly three-axle LTs of the 1930s which had operated the route up to that time; following a spell with RFs, it was finally converted to double-deck operation in May 1963, using the RT type. Most of Sutton High Street would be pedestrianised by November 1978, upon completion of a gyratory traffic scheme. *Dave Edwards*

Above: Now demoted from Green Line duties by LCBS but still in a base Lincoln green with its new owner's lemon lettering and logo, RCL2221 waits at the 'Cosy Corner' stop by Chart Lane, Reigate, on route 414 (Horsham–West Croydon) during March 1972. Following replacement of the type by OPO vehicles in 1977, RCL2221 would return to LT in March 1978 and has subsequently been used as a mobile cinema/exhibition bus, even appearing in my present home city of Exeter in 1989 promoting the use of 'green' fuels!. It is currently based at Acton with LRT Central Distribution Services, in the form of a mobile travel-information centre. *Roy Hobbs*

Left: Green Line route 709 was the last to employ crew-operated Routemaster coaches, these being replaced by Leyland National single-deckers in May 1976 — some four years after the previous conversion, of route 715 (Guildford–Hertford) in April 1972. Here RCL2237 stands outside Godstone (GD) garage awaiting its next turn of duty to London (Baker Street) on 9 March 1972. Following the changeover the remaining vehicles would be transferred to bus work, as seen in the previous view. Whilst a number of these former Green Line coaches have survived with other operators, including two exported to Canada, RCL2237 met its end at a Yorkshire breaker's yard in 1985. Godstone garage was opened by ESTC in 1925 and closed in July 1990, the site being given over to housing development. *R. C. Riley*

Below: Whilst operating from Staines (ST) garage, now closed, modernised Green Line RF99 is seen working a route 701 duty through its home town in the early 1970s. The absence of roof-mounted destination boards will be noted, these having been phased out soon after the separation from LT, when LCBS assumed responsibility for these services. Route 701 had its origins in a Green Line service from Ascot to Oxford Circus that started in September 1930. By July 1933, as route A, this had been extended across London to Gravesend and in 1937 was renumbered A1, before being disrupted by World War 2; after a period of stop-gap operation during the period 1940-2 it was withdrawn, being reintroduced in June 1946 as route 701, which survived until withdrawal (without replacement) in October 1975. At this time Staines was the focus for three other Green Line routes — the 702 to Sunningdale and the 718 and 725, which terminated at Windsor. *John May*

Left: Following the return to Chiswick in 1948 of the various body-shop technicians employed at Reigate (RG) garage during and immediately after World War 2, the special service from Reigate to Chiswick, and later Aldenham, works was enhanced to cater for those who lived or had settled in Surrey. Over the years a variety of redundant vehicles was employed, ranging from 'Bluebird' LT1425 in 1949 through STL, 10T10, 2RT2, RTL and GS types to standard RMs and RMAs based at Shepherds Bush (S) garage. This long-standing operation finally ceased in 1986 following the transfer of the LT Engineering Division to Bus Engineering Ltd. Here GS62, now preserved, waits to pick up its passengers at the Woodhatch collection point at around 6.30am one morning in June 1972. *Roy Hobbs*

Left: Chelsham (CM) garage, near Warlingham, was constructed in January 1925 for East Surrey. Given the various rationalisations that have occurred in recent times, its eventual closure — in April 1990 — was a foregone conclusion, and the site is now occupied by a national supermarket chain. RF69, originally a Green Line coach, is pictured on the garage forecourt in May 1973. It features the second-stage LCBS livery, retaining the basic dark Lincoln green inherited from LT but with lemon-yellow window surrounds, fleetnames and fleetnumbers in place of the cream and gold used previously. This vehicle would remain in service until May 1976. *Mike Harries*

With steam escaping from its radiator relief valve, RT4755 appears not to be in too good a shape as it stands at the Tadworth terminus of route 406 in July 1973. This short working of the route (originally designated 406A) between Kingston and Tadworth involves lengthy climbs through the North Downs which can be quite taxing for a bus with a full load. Until August 1974 the stand, alongside Tadworth station in The Avenue, was used also as the terminus for route 416 to Esher, shown earlier. Behind RT4755 can be seen the photographer's vintage 1929 Austin Seven Swallow. *Kevin McCormack*

Left: Sold RLH35 is seen near Leatherhead, conveying members of the Reigate Grammar School Scout Group, possibly returning from a camping expedition, in the summer of 1973. Of the 76 class members, this particular RLH was unique in being sold directly to the school in 1970, rather than passing through the hands of a dealer. A good proportion of the type were sold on for further use in various capacities, their low overall height being an obvious advantage; well over half are known to have been exported to North America, whilst a number are now in Western Europe. RLH35 was sold again in January 1986 and was last heard of in 1992 in the ownership of one Marco Ghidorzi in Basel. *Kevin McCormack*

Above: On one of the numerous Sunday excursions run for staff by LT's Central Area garages to various coastal resorts during spring and summer, RT698 of Seven Kings (AP) garage is pictured near the 'Prince Albert' at South Earlswood on a rather quiet A23 Brighton Road during a spring day in 1973. Following the 1947 Transport Act, LT was permitted to carry out private-hire operations within a 100-mile radius of its London HQ by arrangement with the BTC, along with the previously accepted staff outings. However, this concession was removed in 1953, whereafter only the staff excursions were allowed to continue. This regulation remained in force up to the time of privatisation in the mid-1990s, when the rules relating to all independent operators were applied. *Roy Hobbs*

Left: The first 25 vehicles of the RF class were built in 1951 to replace the LTC-type three-axle AEC Renown coaches forming the basis of the Private Hire fleet and were painted in the attractive colour scheme seen here on preserved RF10, passing the 'Prince Albert' (now refurbished as a hamburger restaurant) while participating in the HCVC run to Brighton in May 1975. Due to existing regulations they were constructed to a length of 27ft 6in, but all subsequent RFs were 30ft long. As with earlier Private Hire vehicles, observation windows were fitted at roof level and public-address equipment was installed. A further 15 8ft-wide luxury coaches, designated RFW, were introduced at the same time for long-distance contract work, these bearing 39-seat bodies by Eastern Coach Works and similarly finished. *Roy Hobbs*

Left: Crawley local service 426A collects a further set of passengers outside the 'White Hart' in the old town centre on 31 May 1975 before heading for Ifield. Red AEC Merlin MBS34 was among a number of these vehicles, hired by LCBS from LT between 1974 and 1976, that operated from various garages, including Crawley, Reigate and Dorking. Reigate's route 430 was the first in the Country Area to use green examples of the type, in November 1968, when experimental Autofare passenger-operated equipment, issuing either a 6d (2½p) or 1s (5p) flat fare, was installed; this proved troublesome in service and was later abandoned. The Merlins themselves also revealed shortcomings and most were soon replaced by Leyland Nationals, the majority going to breakers' yards, but a number were sold to operators in Northern Ireland and Australia. Less than a handful remain active in preservation in this country. *Colin Brown*

School-journey variations were a feature of a number of routes operated by LCBS and its predecessor, former Green Line RF202 being shown in rural surroundings near Oxted whilst on just such a working of route 464 on 27 May 1975. Several of the class used on Green Line services were downgraded from February 1973 onwards, following their replacement by new Leyland Nationals. RF202 had initially reverted to bus livery but was later restored to the modernised Green Line scheme first introduced in 1966, being retained by the company for working excursions and special services. It was subsequently sold on into private preservation and is currently based in Cornwall, bearing the registration and identity of RF141. *Colin Brown*

RT2872 heads south past Kingston railway station towards Chessington Zoo with a route 65 duty from Ealing in July 1975. This had originally continued through to Leatherhead from Chessington but was cut back in November 1968, when route 71, originally running from Richmond to Kingston, was extended to Leatherhead in replacement. Latterly worked by RMs from Kingston (K) garage, the 71 was similarly shortened in March 1979. In recent times this road has been covered by route 465 (Fulwell–Dorking), currently operated by Tellings-Golden Miller employing the ubiquitous Dennis Dart single-decker. *Dave Brown*

Right: Judging by the absence of traffic in Dorking High Street on 1 July 1975, this photograph must have been taken early in the evening, when most routine traffic had dissipated. Although long-distance journeys are now generally catered for by the M25, considerable traffic still passes through the town centre along the A25, due to the impracticality of providing an inner ring road in the east–west direction. Having left the 'White Horse' stop, RF255 heads for Guildford on route 425, which in July 1973 had been extended from Dorking to Redhill to replace original route 439, itself extended back to Guildford (whilst retaining the Newdigate loop section from Dorking) at the same time. Following further adjustments the 439 would finally be withdrawn in October 1986. RF255 is now privately preserved in Metrobus livery at Southborough in Kent.
Michael Furnell

Right: Former Green Line RF191, now relegated to ordinary bus work, finds itself pressed into service once more on Green Line route 708 from Hemel Hempstead to East Grinstead, being seen passing through Godstone village, at the crossroads of the A22 and A25, on 31 May 1976. Having been upgraded in October 1966, it has now returned to standard bus livery, with roofboard brackets removed. The southern section of the 708 was withdrawn in April 1978 and replaced by route 719, which was diverted to East Grinstead from its former terminus at Wrotham. However, this adjustment was short-lived, and the route was similarly cut back to Victoria in October 1979, being replaced (in part) by a weekday 409 Express bus service from Croydon.
Michael Furnell

Above: On a somewhat overcast and rainy 18 February 1977, RT986 passes along the A22 close to Blindley Heath, between South Godstone and Lingfield, with a route 409 duty to Forest Row in East Sussex. The use of a numbered side blind in the intermediate destination box will be noted. The roof dome also bears witness to discontinuance of the one-time practice of using a special vehicle — often a converted redundant double-decker — to remove overhanging branches along the line of route. The East Grinstead–Forest Row section would survive until October 1979, its withdrawal removing London Country's last connection with East Sussex. *Michael Furnell*

Right: On a route 218 short working to the town terminus, RF527 pulls away from the 'Orleans Arms' at Esher during April 1977. This route and the 219 (Kingston–Weybridge) were the last throughout the former LT area (including that of LCBS) to employ the RF type, the survivors being ceremonially taken out of service at the close of March 1979, after which Leyland Nationals took over. RF527 was one of a number of its class to bear the 'LONDON TRANSPORT' fleetname without underlining, as applied also to RT-type vehicles in their final years of service. *Dave Brown*

Left: RT3461 passes along Limpsfield Road, Hamsey Green, on a 403 journey from Chelsham in June 1977. This bus was one of only six of its type to be painted in NBC leaf green, the others being RTs 604, 981, 1018, 2230 and 2367, the last two as driver-trainers. This was the result of a vehicle shortage, which required their recertification for a short period before the type's final removal from LCBS service. It will be noted that the main 'via' box is carrying an RMC blind, rendering the route-number aperture superfluous. Of these final six vehicles, all four in passenger use have since survived into private preservation. The photographer has upgraded his personal transport since an earlier picture and now owns the Morris Minor on the left of this view! *Kevin McCormack*

Above: On a wintry March day in 1978, RCL2244 deposits a passenger at the Goodwyns Farm Estate stop, south of Dorking, whilst on a route 449 duty. It is interesting to reflect that when this service was first introduced in March 1950, initially to the other terminus at Chart Downs, one of the single-manned 20-seat Leyland Cubs was used. With the continuing expansion of the two large council estates at its opposite ends, higher-capacity vehicles were introduced progressively over subsequent years, with the end result seen here. However, with the onward march of car ownership, the two communities no longer have a dedicated local service but are catered for by Arriva route 93 from Horsham. Incidentally, RCL2244 and its route are the subject of an excellent diecast model by EFE. *Roy Hobbs*

Left: RM1005 on route 27 (Highgate–Teddington Station) passes the former RF506 on route 235 (Richmond–Richmond Hill) during September 1978 on the approach to the station. By this time Continental Pioneer had taken over the 235, formerly in the hands of Isleworth Coaches, which had assumed the route following an overtime ban by LT employees in 1966, using a redundant LT RTL. Having employed this type initially, Continental Pioneer later adopted the RF shown but eventually gave up the operation in September 1980, whereafter Richmond Hill was served once again by LT, with a diversion of route 71. After a period in store RM1005, re-registered ALC 290A due to the value of its earlier mark, has returned to service on Sovereign London route 13 (Golders Green–Aldwych) and may become one of the last of its type in service. *Roy Hobbs*

Left: Kingston bus station, which, with its adjoining garage, was demolished in August 2000, is the subject of some activity as routes 218 and 219 await their next departures during September 1978. RFs 437 and 502 are the vehicles in view, with the LT roundel flap on the latter in the open position, revealing the radiator filler cap. A further six months were to elapse before the type disappeared from LT service on the two routes shown. First introduced in 1951, the class included several which would see over 26 years of service. A new terminal area has since been established in Cromwell Road, alongside the railway and opposite the original garage site. *Roy Hobbs*

Close to the end of its association with Leatherhead, RM975 waits in the town centre during its last few days of operation, on the final lap of a route 71 journey to the garage terminus. As mentioned previously, the route was shortened to terminate at Surbiton from 31 March 1979, after which red double-deck buses would no longer visit the town on a regular service. A replacement single-deck route 265, operated by the BL type (Bristol LH6L), was introduced at the same time between Leatherhead and Kingston, with a Sunday extension to Richmond, but was itself withdrawn in September 1980. RM975 would be sold by LT to Barnsley breakers in January 1987. *Roy Hobbs*

Below: During the final week of RF operation, in March 1979, RF314 collects its passengers from the stop at the bottom of Esher High Street on the old A3 while LCBS RP18, probably on Green Line route 715 to Guildford, waits at the stand opposite. This particular RF was amongst 25 of the class recertified for further use on Kingston-based routes 218 and 219, having latterly been employed on Reigate–Chiswick/Aldenham staff duties. It was unique in retaining, on its return to passenger use, the twin foglamps fitted during this period. Also evident is a further example of the wooden 'Keston' shelters adopted by LT for use in outer-suburban and country areas, many of which replaced the classic Pick-designed art-deco steel-and-glass waiting shelters familiar throughout LT territory during the 1930s and '40s. *Roy Hobbs*

Right: The railway bridge at Redhill over the main Brighton Road (A23), known locally as the 'Reading Arch', is featured here with restored former Tilling open-staircase AEC Regent ST922 heading for Brighton on the May 1980 HCVC run. This merits inclusion as it repeats a scene familiar in the late 1940s, when Reigate garage operated three of these, both in service and for driver training; at that time ST868 could regularly be found on route 430, on which your author travelled frequently. ST922 was discovered in a Hertfordshire scrapyard, where it languished for several years after disposal in May 1955. Latterly a staff mobile canteen, it was rescued by a preservationist, the late Prince Marshall. Having undergone an extensive and very costly restoration, it first returned to service in April 1972 on route 100, carrying tourists around the West End and to LT's Covent Garden museum, and continued to operate this service for several years before retiring to its present home at Cobham Bus Museum, near Weybridge. *Roy Hobbs*

Left: During January 1979 a large cavity opened in the A307 road at Petersham, between Ham Common and Richmond, due to subsidence caused by an underground spring. The road remained completely closed until September 1980 while repairs were effected, and during this time route 65 was worked in two sections, as were routes 71 and 265, with passengers having to walk the intervening ¼ mile or so around the obstruction. The 'Dysart Arms' became the terminus of the northern section, where RM1040 is seen during May 1980 taking on board passengers who have skirted the 'Petersham Hole' on foot from the south. Because of the length of time taken to solve the problem, local residents held a street party in Petersham to mark a year's existence of 'The Hole'! *Roy Hobbs*

Above: As mentioned earlier, a feature of LT's spring and summer operations from the immediate postwar era onwards was the running of excursions to coastal resorts and elsewhere. Cafés/pubs at three principal locations in Surrey were used regularly for midway refreshment stops. However, with the closure of a section of the Brighton Road in the late 1950s, as a result of the expansion of Gatwick Airport, those at Povey Cross and Lowfield Heath became unavailable, leaving only the 'Thorns' (now the 'Air Balloon') public house at Horley. This continued to be used until around 1980, when local restrictions prohibited further visits. In May 1980, during what was probably the final season, a large group of Routemasters on staff outings, including RMs 2119, 492, 357 and 2205, wait to continue their outward journey. *Roy Hobbs*

On 1 April 1989, to celebrate its establishment as an independent operating unit within London Buses, South London Transport (now Arriva London South) ran two return journeys to Godstone on route 159, these being extended from Thornton Heath. Coincidentally, this marked a few months over 60 years since the route bearing this number ran on Sundays and Bank Holidays from Camden Town to Godstone for Thomas Tilling. RML2305 was an appropriate choice for the duty, having been temporarily allocated to Godstone in 1965 (as depicted on page 16). It is seen here on an outward working passing through Godstone village on its way to the 'Hare & Hounds' stop adjacent to Godstone Green. The bus is currently in the ownership of London General and until recent times operated on route 11, now converted to OPO using Volvo B7TLs with striking Wright bodywork. *Roy Hobbs*

As an indication of the changes that have taken place since the main period covered in this album, red Dennis Trident TA28 is shown on a route 405 working heading for Redhill bus station along Princess Way on 8 April 2002. Following the withdrawal in April 2001 of LCBS successor Arriva from most services in east Surrey, former LT Country Area route 405 was put out to contract by London Buses, which allocated the service initially to Connex Bus of Beddington. This introduced regular red buses to Redhill for the first time in many years. The service was usually maintained by Dennis Dart single-deckers, but when one of these was unavailable a Trident double-decker was substituted. *Roy Hobbs*

Index of Locations

Full details of Ian Allan Publishing
titles can be found on
www.ianallanpublishing.com
or by writing for a free copy of our latest catalogue to:
Marketing Dept., Ian Allan Publishing,
Riverdene Business Park,
Molesey Road, Hersham KT12 4RG.

For an unrivalled range of aviation, military, transport and
maritime publications, visit our secure on-line bookshop at
www.ianallansuperstore.com
or visit the Ian Allan Bookshops in

Birmingham
47 Stephenson Street, B2 4DH; Tel: 0121 643 2496;
e-mail: bcc@ianallanpublishing.co.uk

Cardiff
31 Royal Arcade, CF10 1AE; Tel: 02920 390615;
e-mail: cardiff@ianallanpublishing.co.uk

London
45/46 Lower Marsh, Waterloo, SE1 7RG; Tel: 020 7401 2100;
e-mail: waterloo@ianallanpublishing.co.uk

Manchester
5 Piccadilly Station Approach, M1 2GH; Tel: 0161 237 9840;
e-mail: manchester@ianallanpublishing.co.uk

and (aviation and military titles only) at
The Aviation Experience, Birmingham International Airport
3rd Floor, Main Terminal, B26 3QJ; Tel: 0121 781 0921
e-mail: bia@ianallanpublishing.co.uk

or through mail order by writing to:
Ian Allan Mail Order Dept.,
4 Watling Drive, Hinckley LE10 3EY.
Tel: 01455 254450.
Fax: 01455 233737.
e-mail: midlandbooks@compuserve.com

You are only a visit away from over 1,000 publishers worldwide.

Back cover: Marking the earlier allocation of evening and Sunday journeys on Surrey County Council-contracted route 522 to Wandle Buses, two special trips were run on 8 May 1988 using RML2615 of Stockwell (SW) garage. These duties had previously been covered by London Country (South West), which continued operating the remaining weekday services on parent route 422. Substituting for the usual DMS from Sutton (A) garage, RML2615 is seen leaving Reigate (Bell Street) with the final working. *Roy Hobbs*